The Impeccable Journey
by Gary Bate

The Impeccable Journey

Copyright Gary Bate September 2020

Cover design by Wilma Lensink

ISBN 9781838197193

Published September 2020

Blue Light Publishing

Contents

Introduction

I wasn't going to write another book (according to my mind) but I suddenly had a realisation (as one does) and I realised that there is no peace unless there is peace of mind and there is no peace of mind unless one lives an impeccable life.

If you don't live an impeccable life, there will always be something on your mind and you will by-pass this life whilst you are occupied with what's on your mind. This book takes you on the journey to becoming impeccable...

Anyone can learn the philosophy of enlightenment – that's easy if you know where to find it. The difficulty is putting it into practice in your life (living it) because it requires that you radically, yet gradually, change yourself into becoming a completely different person.

Enlightenment is not an adding to your personality; it's a purging of your personality – purging yourself of all your limitations. It's like getting into a balloon basket with many sandbags in it and gradually throwing them out one by one.

Please note this book is a complete read for beginners and for those who think they are advanced on the path. You will always get what you are ready to hear. If, after reading it, you want more 'meat on the bones' so to speak, I suggest you read my other titles starting with 'We are here to know ourselves'.

It's not the number of words in a book that matters.

You cannot judge value by how big a book is. It's the contemplations that the words stimulate that matters.

We are all 'works in progress', otherwise we wouldn't be here. How we live our lives from now on is up to us - please let's do it super-consciously.

In 'We are here to know ourselves' there's a chapter called A New Life. This book is my new life ~ Gary Bate

Oneness

This term has been talked about for a while now and there's a question mark over how well it's understood and moreover, how well it's accepted and lived.

Oneness does not mean that we are not individuals, for our Soul journeys are all unique. But oneness does mean that we are not separate from others and from all life for that matter.

Separation is the illusion and it's the cause of all mental aberration (conflict) on this planet. If the 'powers that be' understood and accepted that they are not separate from those they wish to have absolute control over, then we'd all live in a blissful World. But no, absolute power is their aphrodisiac.

Now I could dribble on about this, but I've decided to write this book in a deliberate fashion, making it short, punchy and powerful. I hope you enjoy it.

Precious Soul

Your Soul is precious to you because it has all of your memories from the very beginning of your existence. It is your book of this life and of all of your lives.

It can be opened but ordinarily it is unavailable to your conscious mind in every lifetime. This is because you would be paralysed by all those memories and thus be unable to function in your new life. Imagine being born with your whole history of all your lives to contend with! You'd need to be very wise to not be a crazed babe!! So there's a reason for this veiled environment...

Your Soul 'nudges' you at various times in your life because it is striving for 'completion' and you have programmed it in between incarnations. The reason you did this, is your evolution, as the overall purpose of your life is to evolve yourself.

Notice I said that you had programmed your Soul. Therefore I am saying that you are not your Soul.

There is only consciousness (energy) and all else has been born from that, including your Spirit and your Soul. Along with your mind and your body, these are accumulations to what you are, but they are not what you are.

Your Spirit is like a drop of water and the Great Spirit is the whole sea. Your Soul is individual and unique and it is linked energetically to your Spirit. No two people have the same journeys or the same unfinished business in their Souls. You are a unique *Oneness*.

Judgment

We do not look at situations in our lives and just accept them for what they are. Similarly, we do not look at other people and just accept them for how they are.

We have analytical minds that have their foundations in our pasts and so we are almost conditioned to judge every situation and every person. We have this awful tendency to analyse and judge everything.

Your mind knows nothing about the now moment because it is never present in the now moment – it is always coming from somewhere in your past. And yet the only truth is what's happening right now! What you are thinking is an analytical hypothesis of your reality.

As for the future, all we've got to go on is the patterns of what's happening right now and what's occurred very recently. All that's ever been created has come from our minds, so the plans of the 'powers that be' will definitely become the future days upon this World unless we, the people, wake up and stop them.

The sci-fi movies give great insights into the future as well as being mainly good entertainment. Many clues to the future are easily joined together, some being more obvious than others.

In the context of an impeccable life, there is no judgment in the psyche (mind) of an impeccable person, for all judgment is coming from one's past biases, which are weeded out by 'super-conscious' people. Indeed, in the context of the impeccable journey, there are no such limitations in one's mind.

Judgment has no place in an advanced consciousness; advanced being a person who has learned to mirror the Divine. If God ever judged anything or anyone, nothing would exist in the next moment. Life exists because it's not judged by the source of all life.

Judgment is consistent with an emotional mind caught up in polarised thinking. Thinking in terms of oneness is the end of all judgment.

Everybody is consciously or unconsciously pursuing their own happiness in life, even though you may struggle to comprehend how they can possibly derive happiness from their state of mind! And everybody is doing what they consider to be right, even though you would judge it wrong for them. With this in mind, how can you possibly judge anyone anymore?

You never know what the Soul of another needs to learn in order for them to grow or what brings them their greatest gift — joy.

Responsibility

I have unashamedly nicked this from Sadhguru because I think it's such a good contemplation and because there's nothing new under this sun (it's all been said before by someone else).

These people who enforce their copyright are ignorant. You can't say or even think anything that some enlightened being hasn't said or thought before. So nobody really has a right over anything that is said or thought.

I hereby give credit to Sadhguru for part of this chapter and further I recommend that everyone do his online inner engineering course, it's excellent.

Responsibility is basically misconstrued. It means to be able to respond (response-able). If you say you are not responsible then you are not able to respond. But if you accept that your responsibility is unlimited then you are always able to respond to any situation. How you respond is up to you.

Thus Sadhguru teaches that there's a difference between responsibility and action. Even a non-action is an action. You can do nothing and be responsible.

The point is to always have an unlimited mind and thus to always be in a position where you have the ability to respond, even if that results in no action.

Just add it to your truth list - "I am responsible for everything and everyone in my life". "I accept reality for how it is right now". "I live here and now".

The problem with this World is the few tyrants who assume the masses are utterly irresponsible (useless eaters) and thus they have to dictate to us how we should live our lives, as if it's their decision, which it is not.

Having a superiority complex is delusional. Thinking you can design the World in your own image is delusional. Thinking other people are upon this world to be your slave is delusional. Working for these delusional people is delusional. Not standing up for yourself by allowing crazed psychopaths to pull the strings is delusional. Is it possible that delusional, crazed, psychopaths can steer this ship? It's happening now because people are not standing up and saying NO.

Detachment

I want to discuss inclusiveness and detachment with you, even though I have no fixed opinion on either of these opposites.

Many teachers teach detachment and some teach being inclusive of others. Some hide away in caves, as far away from social consciousness as possible; and others revel in their popularity from the love they exude to all.

Some teach that the height of human expression is joy and a blissful death and others teach that following your joy should lead you to enlightenment and a natural ascension.

It is not for me to say who and which of these self-proclaimed masters is correct, for I do not make such claims. However, I will say this:

I believe the Divine is unlimited in nature and that we are here to become like the Divine. I did not come here to die. I came here to explore a better option.

As we grow and become more loving, that may or may not affect our popularity and we may become more inclusive or more detached. I think it's really quite irrelevant. What do you think?

There are teachers and gurus who have many fans and followers and there was apparently a man, a master, who apparently had only 12 disciples. Ponder that.

Popularity never proved anyone correct. That is not to

say that a popular teacher is incorrect. A person who is on *The Impeccable Journey* may become popular but they may also have to walk alone for many years. Such a person is at ease with self whether they walk alone or they are in company.

Please do not make a religion out of everything, but rather strive to master all of your compulsive behaviours. There's no need to strive to be detached from others or to be involved with them; it's a no thing. It's how you are that counts.

It's Time

I have no doubt that enlightenment is all wrapped up with our understanding of time. It's so easy for any of us to get caught in the trap of thinking time is linear; the effects of which are clear to see in everyone's faces and lives...

Picture this – you're standing on a river bank watching the river. You notice that the current is meandering along close to the bank, but as your view expands towards the centre of the river, you see how much faster the river progressively goes the further it moves away from the bank. You get into the river and move with the current closest to the bank. Eventually, you get out of the river and walk back to your starting point and re-enter! Why have you done this?

The river of course is the river of life and it is constantly flowing. Each identifiable change in current speed represents another time flow (a different plane or dimension). You of course are you – the only truth there is! You are Energy manifest as Spirit & Soul, observing the river until you immerse yourself in it; then you are Spirit & Soul & Body having experiences in the waters of this time flow.

Because of a lack of real education and training, you get trapped in this current of life and you think it's the only reality there is. Thinking you are just a body, you believe you are on a collision course with your own death; so you create your own death with your own mind. You re-emerge from the river, realise you need to change something and go back to re-enter yet again to change it. What is it you need to change?

How many times have we all done this before? How many times have we died, gone to the Light and been re-born to our past to change something in our Souls? What are we not getting? Wisdom! What are we not understanding? The reason some people can predict the future is because they are remembering it...

There is a very good movie called The Butterfly Effect, which tracks the life scenarios of a young man who keeps going back in time and he keeps changing his actions around a certain incident that occurred. It's very interesting to see how his life plays out with each change of attitude and it makes one appreciate how each decision we are making is affecting our lives. Of course this is consistent with quantum physics and parallel Worlds theory, on the basis that all times exist simultaneously in the now.

The point of including this chapter is just to get you to think outside of the box of your seemingly fixed reality. There really is no truth other than you and what you are creating. You are the truth; it is your life playing out in front of your eyes, which is created by your mind consciously or unconsciously.

Ulterior Motives

This is an extremely serious topic because it relates to our shadowy, phantom self, which creeps into all areas of our lives. Ulterior motives are masked lies.

People think there's a lot to say about enlightenment but they're incorrect – there's not much to say; there's just a few qualities to live true to.

Ulterior motives are 'ever-present' in a consciousness that is always trying to manipulate and control others.

You will not escape them in your own life (it's partly the reason you are here). You can only become aware of them and retire one tentacle at a time...

Unconditional love is the absence of ulterior motives.

Some ulterior motives are plain funny because they are so obvious and often both parties involved will laugh it off; but many are subtle and operate below full consciousness and some are so very subtle that a degree of self-mastery and self-honesty are required to keep them in check.

You cannot be a genuine, real person until all of your motives are pure and seen.

The examples are many so it's not for me to give you examples as you will have many of your own. It's like slowly weeding a large over-grown garden.

You will say less when you have finished weeding...

The Purpose of Ego

Everyone has heard the term Ego and most people also know the term Altered-ego. The latter is obviously an alteration of the former.

So is God an Ego or an Altered-ego? Do we have Ego or Altered-ego or both?

The terms have got somewhat confused, so it's safer to either drop them or go with what is commonly known as Ego, which is the Phantom (shadow) Self.

There are 'images' and there is that which gives life to those 'images'. The experience here is image consciousness, meaning living as various images and ignoring the fact that you are that which gives life to them.

We are the experiencer of the experiences; not the identity of them.

So Ego self is image self and it gives an orderly sense of experience, albeit illusionary. For instance, thinking you are your body and acting as if you are, is egotistical.

The most successful people often have the strongest Ego's, but of course that only pertains to the temporary 'Worldly success'.

We came to this World to be Ego, to experience Ego, to take image consciousness to the extremes and we've done that. And yet it continues, because we continue to feed it...

Can greed feed it? Can feeling superior feed it? Can wanting to feel special feed it? Can wanting others to pity you feed it? Can self-importance feed it? Can feeling powerful feed it? Can compliments feed it? Are you getting this?

Ego generally works for you in this World because this is an 'image-conscious' World. It only seemingly works against you when you're not getting what you want and often you don't know what you want!

So Ego is necessary to function in this life. Without it you won't have any Worldly success in your life. You won't try to look your best to attract a partner. Without Ego you probably wouldn't get married and or have a family. You probably wouldn't have gone to college and pursued a career. Without Ego, you wouldn't have done most of the things that you've done.

The *Purpose of Ego* (the phantom, shadow self) is to give us experiences to ultimately make us wiser...

Overcoming Addiction

We are feeling beings and the purpose of our experiences is to feel and capture the emotion. But there's a trap and it's constant repetition. This causes us to be chemically addicted (in the body) to our experiences.

To understand how this works and what you might be addicted to, just ask yourself the question - is there anything or anyone or any activity that I simply can't give up?

When we think about addiction we think of the obvious ones, such as drugs and alcohol. But people also get addicted to food, entertainment, sex, pastimes and other people, like family members, politicians, pastors and teachers; indeed, any dominant personality. Not to mention our animals...

Who or what can't you give up? The underlying reason is always emotional and thus emotional addiction is the biggest addiction.

The fact that we are all addicted to something or someone, means we are all vulnerable to being controlled. Nefarious elites know this and they control us through our emotional bodies.

Is there an individual resolve? Yes if it's done correctly and if one invests time in it.

Regular meditation (deep contemplation) helps with emotional resolution (wisdom), which in turn slowly moves one's kundalini energy out of the lower chakras on its journey up to the so-called third eye (the seventh chakra).

I am not aware of any other resolve to what is the biggest disease and killer of all – emotional addiction.

All of the gurus that I've listened to say that we can improve the quality of our lives and even experience bliss, but that we cannot avoid death. Are they correct?

Most of us are not bad people but all of us are emotionally addicted and this is what makes us sick and eventually takes us to the grave (in most cases). To my mind, enlightenment and the rejuvenation of one's body, is achieved by moving beyond emotional addiction. Of course there's only one way to know that and that's to prove it to yourself.

We came into this World to experience emotion and to move away from it as wiser souls, but instead we got caught up in it and we kept repeating the same or similar experiences.

The whole structure and mindset of this World is conducive for this to happen. Without the right knowledge we are doomed from the outset.

We should be hot on the heels of new experiences instead of lingering in the emotions of the past. The latter is why we age...

Overcoming Emotions

If you google emotional mind hooks you'll come to an article and simple exercise of mine, which you might like and which might help you.

Emotions are an orderly sense of experience. Life is a succession of never-ending experiences and it all happens *inside* of you. You experience and you feel the emotion of it.

We are supposed to be constantly embarking upon new experiences or feeling the emotions on the other side of them. But due to the the nature of our compulsive, addicted minds, we have fallen into lives of repetition and emotions that have grown in form. We have lost our ability to reason objectively and replaced it with being emotional and at times out of control.

The emotions are like programs that just run and we're not sharp enough to hit the pause button before the ugliness kicks in. Hitting the pause button is a must.

One of the biggest problems for most of us, is we always want life to be how we want it to be and thus we get emotional if things don't go exactly how we want them to go. We must start to accept reality for how it is and drop this silly idea that it's always got to fit our image and be like we want it to be.

In a deeper sense, repetitive emotions are always a sign of something you don't understand. The trigger has gone off before you've hit the pause button and before you've tried to understand the prevailing situation.

When you decide to invest in yourself, your gains in wisdom will gradually retire your repetitive emotions. My simple exercise will help you...

O go on then I'll put it in this book:

Emotional Mind Hooks by Gary Bate

Let me start by making a bold statement here. It is the molecules of emotion bathing your body cells (via neuro-peptides, hormones and steroids in your blood stream) that are causing disease and ageing in your body. Unless this situation is addressed you will remain on a 'time line' towards the eventual death of your body.

These molecules of emotion are present in your body because of Psychological Stress (refer my previous Chapter) and your own misconceived conclusions from past events. In other words, the events may have passed but you are still running them as emotions in your mind and body because you haven't *owned* them as wisdom.

All that a teacher can do is give you knowledge and disciplines that will lead you into your own 'inner circle'. If you don't 'get it' or you don't 'realise' the wisdom or you choose not to own it by seeking comfort in your past; then that does not fault the teacher, but is evidence that they respect your free will to engage or not to engage them.

I am hereby going to give you a simple exercise that, if you do it, will propel you forward in your evolution.

Step 1

The first thing I want you to do is to find some quiet time on your own where you will not be disturbed. Get a pen and paper in readiness for step 2.

Step 2

Write down every emotion you currently experience in your daily life. Below I have given you a checklist but it is important that you write your own list and NAME each emotion 'out loud' as you write it down. If you are unsure about any on the checklist then close your eyes, ask the question and contemplate upon that emotion. You'll soon know whether it's a part of your psyche or not!

Anger, jealousy, envy, bitterness, regret, feeling lost, lonely, sad, guilt, doubt, betrayal, rejection, hurt, aggressiveness, depressed, fearful, anxious, upset, inadequate, unworthy, shameful, feeling used and /or abused, sympathy, feeling sorry, compassion, feeling responsible for other grown-ups (even if they are your relations), shyness, embarrassment, impatience. Have I missed anything?

Step 3

Add up all of the emotions that you suffer from and arrange them on another piece of paper in the form of a wheel with spokes, naming each emotion in a box at the end of each spoke and leaving a 'free space' in the hub of the wheel.

Step 4

Study your wheel, acquaint yourself with it, name your emotions again and be able to picture your wheel with your eyes closed - this is very important to the process. Please do not go any further until you have accomplished this.

Step 5

In your own time, close your eyes and see your wheel with all of your emotions. You can picture a fairground wheel if you wish, with all of your emotions sitting in the chairs! With your eyes still closed, what you are now looking for is your Emotional Mind Hook that is hooking you into your emotional responses and you are looking to name it in that 'free space' in the hub of your wheel.

What part of your psyche is hooking you up to all of these emotions? What is it? Is it more than one aspect of your personality? Stay in deep contemplation and seek to NAME it and place it at the centre of your wheel. It is not enough to just think about it because you will only come up with another 'surface' emotion. You must go into deep contemplation with your eyes closed and stay with it until you get your answers.

Step 6

Did you fill the space? If not, here are a few probabilities that you may not have considered through your own contemplation. Take each one at a time, close your eyes and place the word at the centre of your wheel and contemplate upon it to see if it fits in with you.

Control, acceptance, approval, assumed responsibility, praise, self-importance, insecurity, victim, know all, liar, cheat, sexual predator, sexual prey, compromise, bully, manipulation, revenge, competitive, hostile, tyrannical, domineering, argumentative, submissive, ridicule, intolerance. Have I missed anything?

All of these Emotional Mind Hooks are just symptoms of a lack of self-love and very apparent in the human condition otherwise we wouldn't be human! They are all merely illusional experiences and collectively they represent the fake aspects of us. What is real in us becomes known when we 'pull the plug' on these illusions. So the hook is the reason for the emotion, it is the cause and the emotions are the symptoms.

Step 7

Now that you are aware of your Emotional Mind Hooks, it is now time to float your past down the river. Close your eyes and picture a black box, a shoebox or something like that. Put a slit in the lid big enough to put folded pieces of paper in. Get a pad of paper in your mind and one by one, write each emotion on a separate piece of paper and put your name on it. One by one, fold each sheet and put them in your box. When you've finished, in big letters, write the word DEMONS on the outside of your box. Now take your box to the riverbank and float it down the river. As you see it disappear out of view, repeat slowly the following affirmation, 3 times: - "I am no longer my past - my past in no more. My demons have gone - they are no longer a part of me".

Step 8

Well done! From this moment forth, every time you experience an emotion, name it, find its hook and challenge it, then box it up and float it down the river. And remember to say the affirmation as it floats out of your life. What is 'in error' with us is what is 'unnamed' in us. To heal we firstly have to reveal.

Incorrect Identities

This is also a very important consideration because the self-branding of incorrect identities is the biggest limiting factor in our lives. We fall from grace and become less divine at our own hands.

The less we say about ourselves the better. We have this nasty habit, almost on auto, of limiting ourselves in almost every sentence we speak. Please stop it!

You are not this, that or the other; you don't even know what you are. So say nothing and be undefined. If you do that you will move closer to the Divine.

How can we ever really define that which is constantly expanding? Any limiting definition makes it static and non-evolving.

"I am always becoming that which I am becoming" is one to use if you have to.

Are you male or female? Are you a doctor or an engineer or a janitor? Are you a mother or a husband? You are none of these really – they are just experiences you are having. Clear up your confusion and stop keep identifying yourself for Christ's sake.

I can't over-emphasise this topic because we foolishly limit ourselves by the identities we give ourselves.

If we don't get on top of our minds, they will bring us down. If we don't make it out of here, it will be for one reason – not enough self-love.

Fantasy or Creation

I don't yet know how true this is, but I heard from an off-World teacher that fantasy is the last mastery in the quest to becoming enlightened.

It has to be seen in the context of training one's mind and mind mastery, because that's the only place fantasy occurs.

I am not going to define it because you all know what a fantasy is. However, having become aware of this teaching, it has surprised me to discover how easily and often subtly we all fall into fantasy. Becoming aware of our fantasies is an art in and of itself. The question in my mind is – is mastery over one's fantasy life simply a matter of stopping all fantasies in their tracks?

There are many teachers who teach conscious creation via creative visualisation (targeted imagination). They teach that you imagine and see yourself achieving your goals as if they've already happened. Many are engaged in such practices and there's much focus on creating fabulous wealth. I am not going to judge the results of such practices, however, it would be nice to hear of someone who has manifested their fabulous wealth from engaging in these teachings...

If the process of creation is deliberate, targeted imagination, then how do we distinguish between that and fantasy?

If you are imagining your cells healing in your body, is

that an example of creation or fantasy?

They say that a fantasy is unlikely to ever happen – how do we know that?

Is it better to dream a beautiful reality than be stuck in your mind in some emotional drama?

I wasn't going to talk about sex or sexuality in this wee book, but it seems fitting here as fantasy plays a big part in both sex and relationships. I distinguish sex from relationships because most women think sex constitutes a relationship and most men don't – another one of the differences between the genders...

Masturbation is the classic fantasy land. I think everyone has at least 'spiced up' their memories for the best hit. But of course, we don't have to work from memory when we can create him or her in our minds.

I'm not going to talk about the games people play and the fetishes they have, because I have zero experience in that area. Clearly fantasy plays a part though.

One area where there can be a huge gulf between reality and mind, is where people are looking for their perfect partner or perfect lover. They have formed the ideal in their mind and just like magic, Mr or Ms wonderful walks into their life. If this newbie ticks some of the boxes from their dream or from their psychic reading, it must be true and the 'newbie' gets overlaid with the fantasy.

Of course it can also be working both ways – fantasies

copulating...

So maybe there's something in the idea, that in the quest for enlightenment (self-mastery), we're not to exclude mastery over our fantasy lives.

Many people get their 'knickers in a twist' about their sex lives or the lack of one. I do think we all place too much importance on this. I find it sad when old men go to the doctor because they can't get an erection.

Should we really be struggling to hang onto what we had when we were younger? Or should we let that energy naturally rise without fighting it?

Is it a great loss to lose your sex life and all that drama and emotion? Or is it a relief? Maybe you can discover new facets of you, if you just let go...

I'm obviously addressing my more mature readers here.

Your life always plays from where your kundalini energy sits in your body. For most men that's the base chakra and for most women it's the sacral plexus (their emotional body). It always sits at the lowest point of a person's consciousness. However, as one let's go of all that drama, emotions, lust and voyeurism; one's kundalini energy naturally gravitates to the higher chakras and creates a 'higher' point of attraction for you. Older and wiser is the phrase.

Isn't is better to be coming from a place of love and to be open to encounter someone who is also coming from the same place, even if that means that such an encounter may never happen?

Let's give up the struggle of trying to hold onto the past, just to satisfy some demons in our heads. If it's not quality what's the point? Let's throw those sandbags out of our baskets!

Two people who love each other

They are two people who choose to come together to share minds and thus realities, to enrich their experiences of life.

They are mindful in their relationship and find reasons to come together rather that excuses to be apart.

They are clean, meaning they are not dragging any 'old partners' around with them. They realise that everyone else in their lives are only there because they want them to be there; otherwise they would be distant memories.

They take responsibility for themselves and care for each other, leaving behind any compromises for financial advantage.

They live for their truth and thus are not concerned by the opinions of others.

They have a sharing attitude – 'what's mine is yours'.

They never use or abuse each other but only give *unconditionally* to one other.

They constantly move forward in their lives, individually and together.

They trust each other because they are brutally honest with each other.

They help each other grow and encourage each other,

delighting in each other's achievements.

They work at letting go of controlling each other in favour of loving each other.

They view love-making as the natural extension of the ecstasy they experience from sharing on all levels, rather than the reason for the relationship itself.

They value their intimacy and keep it sacred, excluding all others.

They know that when one can genuinely forgive then one can always find love whether for the other or for self.

They are flexible and tolerant because they understand that becoming absolutely truthful is a journey that doesn't 'just happen' overnight.

They are two people who love each other.

Forgiveness is wise

We've all done it. We've all judged other people in the past, where they've behaved in ways that doesn't meet with our approval.

We like life to go our way and for other people to behave within our parameters of what we deem to be normal, right, decent, moral, whatever.

We have friends who fit well into our confined minds and some people have enemies, which is an egotistical thing. Some people just have to have an enemy.

If God was to create 'laws of living' we'd all break them and get thrown into the pit! God is lawless.

If we're savvy we'll surely want to mirror the Divine and say, " The Father and I are One".

We cannot change what we have done in the past nor can we change who we have judged in the past, but we can transmute all that old, tied up energy; by finding forgiveness for self and others upon self-reflection. It must be done, otherwise we are stuck.

I could give you many examples from my own life, but I know that you know what I'm talking about because you've just had 'memory flashes' reading this.

My advice is to 'chase down' all of your leaked energy and bring it home through forgiveness. You don't want to be re-incarnated just because you couldn't be bothered to forgive someone or forgive yourself.

But I know you're stubborn and I know you like to have it your way. Attitude really is everything.

It's just a matter of saying, "I forgive you" and "I forgive myself". It's that easy.

Success and Failure

Like I said in the introduction – I am deliberately keeping this book brief because why say in a thousand words what I can say in a hundred?

Success and failure is all about your perception of it, as indeed is everything else in your life. Reality (your life) is your perception of it.

I am writing this as you are reading it (all times exist now). I had no idea you were going to buy my book and I have no idea how many of your friends will buy it or their friends for that matter. So is my book a success or not or do I have to wait and see?

Does the fact that I have written it and published it, make it a success? Does the fact that you are reading it, make it a success? Or does it only become a success when many of your friends and their friends have purchased it?

Who's the judge on success and failure?

In the 'eyes of the World' I have been a failure at being a father, yet I have written 4 books that will help everyone on a Soul level. So do I judge myself as being a success or a failure? Which one is it?

The point is – let's stop all judgment and start to mirror the Divine.

In a greater sense there is only one success and one failure – ascension and death. It's the difference

between getting out of here with a complete Soul or
not. Please contemplate on this and on the fact that
reality is just how you are perceiving it...

Bring joy into your life

I am mentioning this because it has helped me whenever I have felt depressed. I have talked extensively about depression (stress, anxiety) in my other books and I basically said that it's a lack of creative self-expression (a lack of being Spiritual).

Depression is complex but it's basically the result of not living in sync with your Soul. I've found that the best temporary relief from this, is to focus on what brings joy into your life. Thus I have made a list, which includes things like playing music, writing and walking my dogs in nature.

Couldn't we all do with bringing more joy into our lives?

I asked a number of friends, "what brings you joy" and their answers were all very different. Thus it's totally subjective.

What brings you joy? Make a list and bring more of that into your life...

Build a relationship with source

Whatever your concept of God is, doesn't really matter. We all came from a source and that source is therefore the original Mother and Father.

The source energy is in us and we are made out of it, so shouldn't we have some kind of relationship with it?

For me, I just call it my God and I have grown to love my God. It is the one 'energy essence' that's always there for me.

I am conscious of my God and I see it in all things and all life. I talk to it because I perceive it to be real. It does not judge me, but loves me instead. It has been with me for all time and it will continue to be with me wherever I go.

My ambition is to draw closer to it. I refer to it as it because it is neither male or female but both. When all else fails it is still present. I acknowledge my unseen companion and I am conscious enough to know that it provides me with a mirror.

Being 'source conscious' brings a new dimension to your life, a hitherto unseen dimension. When you understand that all life exists because it is allowed to express however it wants to, then you understand that source is providing you with the most clean mirror. It is the mirror of the Divine.

Christ consciousness is the consciousness of a human who perfectly mirrors the Divine source.

A battle for your mind

You mind and your body are indelibly linked and they play each other. There is a feedback loop from your body to your mind and this can be called bodymind.

Your body will always follow your mind, your thinking, but sometimes that thinking is the result of the feedback loop from your body to your mind. You have to get to know who is playing who, but in any event YOU can intercede.

The closeness of your mind and your body is like the closeness of energy and consciousness – they cannot be separated.

The problem is, the body decays and dies if your mind lets it. Likewise, your body resurrects itself and ascends if your mind instructs it so.

We cannot escape our minds and they end up being our worst enemies or our best friends. We have to consciously train them with unlimited thinking...

Be the change you want to see

Many years ago I wrote *The People's Charter for Higher Conscious Living,* which can be viewed at terracharter dot com. In essence, the Charter is a set of principles for impeccable living. Here are those principles for those of you who don't have access to the internet:

1. Treat people with kindness and courtesy.

2. Take responsibility for your actions.

3. Endeavour to be truthful at all times.

4. The incidence of crimes against the people is minimal in a truthful society, as truth comes from one's conscience, it engenders a natural state of morality.

There is no crime against the government as it solely represents the will of the people, which is this Charter.

Prisons are obsolete but secure rehabilitation centres are necessary to educate those who insist on living a life of separatism. They remain the effect of their own actions until they have a change of heart. Common examples of separatism are war, corruption, greed, fraud, child labour, theft, paedophilia, drug & people trafficking, Satanism, rape, murder, covert operations; indeed, any abuse or anti-social behaviour.

5. The welfare of Mother Nature is to be held in the same esteem as the welfare of all people and

everyone has a duty to expose those who put economic gain before her.

6. Technological and engineering advances are to be encouraged and supported especially where they result in the transformation of free energy into useable free energy. Equally, the entrepreneurial spirit is to be encouraged but profiteering at the expense of others or the environment is categorised as separatism.

7. There is one government, one currency and a global task force responsible for a fair distribution of the World's resources. Prejudices are found only in history books.

8. The mainstream media is uncensored and not monopolised.

9. I think it's necessary to state what should be obvious - that we cannot have a unity conscious planet without freedom of speech, unhindered communications and up to the minute disclosure of contact with off/inner World brethren. The super-consciousness here will be our defence against any extra-terrestrial threat and obviously our own terrestrial borders will be a thing of the past, lower consciousness.

10. The new World education model will focus more on where we are going than from whence we came. Hence education will be more research based than historical facts and fiction. Children will be taught quantum physics as well as classic.

11. When a family cannot afford the long-term care of a relative or uninsured medical bills are beyond their means, then 'aid funds' will assist. Many 'pots of money' will be required for the big concerns e.g. Health, Education, Infrastructure.

12. People will voluntarily give a percentage of their income to the Master World Fund, from where monies will be allocated to where they are needed. Giving is a quality of the new conscious people. Public appeals will help raise money for other causes. There is no taxation.

13. As consciousness grows, individuals gradually become their own physicians and help others to do the same. What works for one may work for others, even if there is no objective, scientific proof. The new Healthcare model will give patients a better choice of treatment and this will synergise the health service into a more holistic approach. We cannot have value 2 of the Charter without individuals taking responsibility for their own health and doctors understanding that they are only responsible for the treatments they give to patients. Better and more informed choices, transparent risks, exacting protocols, shared responsibility; is the way to go.

14. As this is a Charter for Higher Conscious living, it must include making available the knowledge for everyone to at least have the opportunity to evolve themselves and realise their highest potentials. I believe that the content of this Charter and the knowledge I have made

available at www.whatstress.com, provides a good starting platform to work from.

15. The end goal for an evolving species is the movement away from self-interest to the motivation that benefits the whole. Currently we live in a world that sacrifices anyone and anything that stands in the way of the self-interest of the few. This is what needs to change and each and everyone of us needs to look at our own motivations ~ Gary Bate.

Changing ourselves is just as important as cleansing our environment. Higher conscious principles for daily living should become the aspiration of individuals and eventually form the basis of a 'People's Charter'. This is the genuine, loving instrument for one World order. We no longer want the existing course that has been steered by the greedy, self-interest of the World's elite.

Having higher conscious principles, as ideals for the human family to collectively work towards, will unite peoples across all faiths. Adhering to such principles, automatically engenders a moralistic state of living and renders religious doctrine unnecessary.

At the individual level, it's a matter of addressing the issues that prevents one from living such an impeccable life. Delving into one's deeper mind for increased self-awareness is the key here.

Time and time again we find that we're on this roller coaster of destructive energy, when we are not being impeccable in our thoughts and actions. Even when we know the truth about an issue in our lives, we still have to do battle with the old consciousness that's fighting for its survival.

It's so important to cement the link between our behaviour and our thoughts, in so much as when we act contrary to our new truth.

Watch your life closely and you will start to see that the egg only sticks to your face when you are being less than impeccable. It is just a matter of tracking your choices to see why undesirable things happen in your life.

Cause and effect is an immutable law. Whether that's karma or karma is the incomplete business in your Soul, doesn't matter because both are unavoidable.

Truth to Evolution

Everybody's truth is different, even if it's just slightly different. This is evidence that truth is subjective in nature. Some will argue for an objective truth but they are just expressing their own truth.

Your truth changes as you evolve and it should be easy to live true to it, but your mind will always try to take you back to the past; because it's built upon the past. When you go backwards in it, you are in your Ego, but when you live true to your new truth, you are operating from your Spirit & Soul.

Living and speaking your truth is a high state of evolution, no matter what your truth is.

Constant change is what your evolution is all about and thus change is a sign that you are evolving. Joint problems tend to be an inability to change. Stagnant evolution is chronic pain in the joints. That's just my conclusion.

People need to understand that truth is subjective and it evolves as you grow. What's true for you today may change tomorrow. Please always keep an open mind. Even the scientists can't agree upon an objective, absolute truth.

One of the things I learned from reading the Nine Faces of Christ, is that truth is individual and it's always evolving, providing we are evolving. There is always a greater order of truth, so we should be cautious when we think we've arrived!

With this in mind, I realised that although the second edition of my first book (We are here to know ourselves) is a complete work in and of itself; having the opportunity to add to it here, doesn't detract from its content but complements it with new material.

You are the Apple of my Eye

I always was but I had never discovered myself because I had never expanded myself beyond being a sleeping void. I contemplated this and in my desire to become more than what I was, I conceived you in my image and lovingly told you to make of me what you will.

You were born from me. Indeed, there was no other way you could come into being for there can be nothing outside of me, because I am all that was and is and will be forever more. You are like a 'Parcel of Delight' to me for you are my children, born of my being and loved into being. I can only love you for love is what I am and therefore the basis of what you are also. I love you – *you are the Apple of my Eye.*

Wow! Haven't we had some adventures together?! You have fed me with all of your experiences and you continue to feed my mind. I know all of your identities, indeed, I know everything that you know and everything that you don't know, from all times. I know this sounds a little intimidating but please remember I simply love you. You are all special to me and equal in my mind – no exceptions and nobody is outside of me.

I am excited about what you will create with the will that is you. You never cease to amaze me, even when you stubbornly insist on the mundane and the repetitive. Perhaps it is fitting for me to remind you that there are no limits in the Kingdom, so please just go for it!

Whatever you decide, I am happy for you, because I

know it is your will and you only ever do what you want to do (otherwise you wouldn't be doing it). I love you regardless of how you decide to express yourself or not express yourself. It makes no difference to me if many of you decide to be lazy, uncreative and stagnate, because I continue to expand anyway – it's the very nature of what I am and I enjoy it. I particularly enjoy creating all those planets and galaxies as future playgrounds for our adventures.

Realities are the limitless outpourings of the mind of God made manifest through the minds of gods.

I am writing this to all my children upon Planet Terra because your planet is evolving and changing and many of you will soon leave for a new playground. Whether you consciously choose to stay or unconsciously choose to leave matters not in the light of all eternity. However, there is much wisdom (for your Souls) to be gained by those of you who choose to stay, witness and experience the unfolding events at this time in your story. So please pay attention to what I have to say.

There are many factors affecting the prevailing conditions upon the planet you call home. There is the effect of other planets like your moon and the potentially destructive effect of rogue planets and asteroids that are now passing through your solar system. I do not interfere with these natural cycles nor do I interfere with how your natural habitat moves in her efforts at cleansing and evolving herself. Nothing is bad as some of you like to think it is but everything is a wilful choice. Please remember that you were all born at the same time and you all have the same power albeit that it is severely subdued in many of you by virtue of your own choices.

In a similar way, I do not interfere in the squabbles and illusionary power games that are the identifying hallmark of your planet. These dramas have been going on for eons! The drive of one god to have power over another god never ceases to amaze me; you seem to delight in creating drama and wars where there was once only peace.

It is true that there are some jealous gods on your planet, who thrive in competition, particularly where it involves the hoarding of more and more money. So fierce has their addiction become that they are blinded to the very basis of their true nature. They kill without hesitation in their pursuit of total planetary domination. The natural cataclysms that you are all experiencing at this moment in your time are not entirely natural. The few of you who are not hard-pressed at working to pay their taxes are aware of their weather modification technology and how they want to be in total control of a World that has about one tenth of its current population.

Some of you might find my words shocking but that is only because you have fell under the spell of very clever mind control techniques that have been designed to keep you ignorant of the true motives of the ones in control. Some of you are even unaware that tyrannical elites control your World and use such techniques, never mind who they are.

Phew it was nice to get that one off my chest! Now let's get to the good news...

Back to you – my beloved:

"If you want to serve then don't single out an individual but serve everyone. Let me serve you as I am doing here; for there is no greater honour. I accept my equality with all beings and that's why I could never worship another individual but could only worship everyone. If somebody requires you to bow or curtsy to them, to serve or worship them or even to kiss their feet, then they just show their ignorance; because they obviously haven't understood the equality of all of us in God. You would be very wise to remove your services from such a mindset" – Gary Bate.

I like the above from your brother because it is exactly what I want you to become – an individual. I love you without conditions, so you are free to be however you want to be, but I also have to say that it pleases me greatly when you create from what I am and serve all others without preference or bias. Then you reflect what I am.

I want you to make mistakes because that provides the friction for you to learn. And gradually I want you to learn and to grow and to polish what you are until you shine like the deity that you are in human form.

The genetic garment you chose was just the friction you needed to learn what you were lacking in wisdom. Always remember that you are not the garment you wear; it is like being in a car and now is the time I want you to stop being a passenger and get into the driving seat and put your foot hard to the floor – let's move it!

Try not to doubt yourself because that is your greatest enemy and don't listen to that critic in your head that says you're not good enough and causes you to feel awful, because I AM telling you that there is nobody greater than YOU, you just need to BELIEVE in you.

I am your loving mother and father - be ONE with me in LOVE.

Death or Ascension

As a father I don't feel it would be right for me to depart this World without giving my offspring the opportunity to benefit from what I know. This is why I started to write 25 years ago and why I still write today.

Everyone you know dies if you don't beat them to it. You never get to know about the ones who never die because you're never around for long enough. To know immortality you've got to be it.

So it is that death is a part of this life and although many memories probably exist in your soul of past deaths and incarnations, they are clearly not available to your conscious mind in this lifetime.

Do we want to approach our demise in an unconscious, beyond the realms of knowing, kind of attitude; or do we want to be more conscious and at least be aware of what we might be faced with?

So what do we have to go on? We have several hundred accounts of near-death experiences where the experiencer started the journey from their body but came back for some reason and we have a few accounts of the after-life from self-proclaimed masters and gurus who are here now or they are now elsewhere.

One common observation from the near-death experiencers is travelling through a tunnel towards a bright light and the feeling of being loved. This is supposedly one's Soul as it travels from where it is usually seated, in your chest (chakra 4), up through the fifth and sixth chakras and exits at the seventh chakra.

Apparently, when one's Soul permanently exits the body, the body dies. It is your Spirit that calls your Soul out, when the body is no longer any use to it. The near-death experiencers started the journey but Spirit changed its mind.

The self-proclaimed masters and gurus also talk about this light and there's a suggestion that it's like a higher frequency mirror World to this World, where all that's here is there and much more. The Light realm is supposedly more exaggerated and more extreme, housing the extremes of good and evil.

Both the self-proclaimed masters and numerous 'out-of-body' experiencers, talk about a realm that one accesses immediately upon leaving the body and before one goes to the Light realm. This realm is referred to as the psychic or astral realm and it's the home of ghosts (people who are emotionally bound to this World). However, it is supposedly a realm where many adventures can be had, for one can travel long distances very quickly due to being in a higher frequency and faster time, than this World.

I am not going to speculate on the validity of religious claims about the after-life, other than to say that there seems to be a common thread that suggests that one manifests (from thought) much more quickly in these higher frequencies.

Science has proven that everything is vibration and our bodies disappear and reappear many times a second.

This is the same for all that appears solid. The idea that other World's exist just outside this frequency and you ascend to one of them when you either lose your body or raise the frequency of it; is more than plausible: it's scientifically sound.

On the basis that consciousness is everything, the theory is – you can only go to where you know and where you are equal to consciously. The Light realm is the highest for people who are of the common, social consciousness of this World. There are even higher realms for those who have moved beyond that, but you can only go to where you know, as it's a conscious journey.

The Light realm then has a similar, yet exaggerated, consciousness to this World. Thus it's a polarised realm of good (saintly) and bad (evil) and all else that thinks in terms of separation. It's not a realm for those who understand and live oneness.

On the balance of probabilities, it seems reasonable to assume that most of the people who die, end up in the Light realm. Home from home but a much faster manifestation – the delights and the ugliness appear much more quickly. So what could be the purpose of this Light realm? Let's take a rational look...

First of all, on the basis that everything is consciousness and resonance, it is reasonable to assume that each frequency (realm, plane) carries a certain consciousness or level of mind.

The Light realm can be considered as a parallel World

for all those who don't have a 'physical' body, whether they are coming from planet Terra or from elsewhere. If there is a Heaven it's clearly not this Light realm. So what's its purpose?

Crudely put – it's a recycling factory of sorts. It's where Soul's park themselves indefinitely, until they once again decide to be born back here to learn more.

There is a relationship going on in the upper echelons of this World and the most evil entities (the demons) in the light. They summon each other and they work together for their individual gains and appetites. As above so below.

I've said much more about this in my first book, 'we are here to know ourselves' and I'm not going to repeat it here. Instead, I'm going to leave this chapter with a couple more contemplations for you:

There is a common theme going on in this World and it's called deception. The 'powers that be' are experts at it. They get away with it because they are also experts at mind control. A great current example is the Covid 19 virus. The patents prove that it was a deliberate ploy to vaccinate (poison) all of us in an effort to radically reduce global population.

The question is – how far does this deception go? Is the Light realm a trap?

There's one way of knowing but you have to have your wits about you. It's whether they are trying to persuade you into doing something, like taking a shot in your arm or coming with them into the light. If someone needs you to do something, then it's deception.

And finally for this chapter. How can you ascend with your body if you have accepted your death? You can't because there is no room in your mind for it. The gurus can talk about being unlimited until the cows come home but they all make the fatal mistake of accepting their own death. That's their flaw.

It's only your physical body that dies and it's only this body that ascends, if you manage to raise its frequency by evolving yourself exponentially.

The Impeccable Journey

What is an impeccable life? It's a life without ulterior motives (lies), without repeating emotions, without judgment, without self-created limited identities, without compulsions and addictions. It's a life of standing up for yourself and living and speaking your truth without diplomacy. It's a responsible life that's lived in the consciousness of oneness.

Only when this is achieved will you have peace of mind and only then will you be fully engaged in life in every now moment.

I just saw a quote by Sadhguru. "You can become truly aware and enjoy every bit of life only if you are constantly aware that you are mortal".

This is where I differ from the gurus. To me, death is a choice, albeit an unconscious choice for most of the population, due to the heavy mind control.

What's the point in doing what you do Sadhguru, if you're going to die anyway?

It takes a lot of self-love to complete *The Impeccable Journey*. Fortunately, this is something that you accrue along the way from doing the work involved to purge yourself. Letting go is the result of wisdom gained.

The choice is always yours. You can live the external, illusionary life, which will leave you without the ability to interact with this last kingdom; or you can take the side of your Spirit and dedicate your life to the internal journey of evolving yourself. Is that not a choice?

Of course you can change paths at any time. Why not today?

When you work diligently on the internal path, you become less reactive to events in the outside World. Right now we have this Covid 19 bio-weapon and all the elite-generated fear-mongering to contend with.

If you truly believe death is a certainty, then what's the problem with you dying now? What's your fear? You're body has died before yet you're still alive now!

It's just your Ego that wants to prolong an illusionary life. The hospitals will help your Ego in that endeavour. It's their job to try and keep your body alive. "Stay at home and Save lives".

Nobody is ever really saved and sick bodies can only be preserved for relatively short periods. You never die. Only your body can die. The question is – do you want to go the same way as the masses (into oblivion) or do you want to explore a better possibility? There's only gain when it comes to evolving yourself.

The brevity of this book is deliberate. Even the best teachers can only take you so far, because the last steps are all experiential.

It is not for me (or indeed anyone) to tell you how to live your life, for your life, just like my life, will be a unique expression of what you are. But knowledge can help you to navigate your life better and in time bring you the pearls of wisdom for your Soul. I am simply 'giving' to you and to all of my readers.

In the very beginning, maybe we all started as 'sparks of intelligent energy' and later we gradually gathered unto ourselves our Spirit, our Soul, our minds and several 'energy bodies' to interact with the different frequency realms of energy.

It is entirely plausible that our evolution is a return journey, which we have been trying to do for eons, but which we have failed at by losing our 'physical' bodies in each 'physical' lifetime.

In any event, wouldn't *oneness* be a better reality than this life of separation? Wouldn't this life be better if we all became real, told the truth and ceased trying to manipulate and control others? Then of course there's living as the true identity rather than identifying with what we experience.

There is no loss in personal evolution, only personal gain. People can argue that the purpose of this life is just to live, but if we're not evolving we're not really living. People go from cradle to grave without ever knowing who or what they really are - living lives as victims to their own out of control minds.

There are no guarantees to the impeccable journey. You could do it; you could purge all lies, all manipulation, all ulterior motives, all judgment, all victimisation, indeed, all limitations; but does that guarantee you a better life? Will you ascend and live in bliss if you put the work in to polish yourself? I think that's a fair question, don't you?

I think peace of mind is the most important thing and that comes with a clear conscience. Conscience is the great regulator and we can't have a clear conscience if we've got all of that aforementioned stuff going on.

So I am an advocate of *The Impeccable Journey* and I will now live true to what I have written. Where will that take me? I really don't care. Where will I end up? I will never 'end up' as I am eternal.

Life is an endless journey and it's a never-ending adventure. To me, it's best that we live it with a clear conscience and the bliss that comes from peace of mind.

Moving beyond the Light realm can't happen whilst you're in it; it can only occur here whilst you still have your body vehicle. Let's make it happen in this lifetime.

~ Gary Bate

Afterword

I guess some people came here to be a footballer or some other vocation that makes them a somebody. There are those who are paranoid about leaving a legacy, even if it's a legacy built upon lies. Reputation and how they go down in history is everything to those people. Then there are those who think life is just about making money, raising a family and dying when it's their turn...

Because we have never really been educated, we have never trained our minds and thus they have become rogue elements, full of compulsive (addictive) behaviours. So what you may think.

Your body can only follow your mind; it has no other choice. So it is that your body's cells suffer at the hands of incorrect, self-created identities and compulsive behaviours coming from your mind. Indeed, they suffer from all of your mental aberration and limitations of your mind.

Your mind gradually becomes the enemy of your body and instead of being life-enhancing, it confuses and decays your body. Ageing and death are coming from your mind and not from a clock. The decay is because your mind, indeed, your personality, doesn't think in an unlimited way.

There are very few ways that you can define yourself that are correct because most self-definitions are limited in nature and thus they are incorrect. Please beware of incorrectly limiting yourself.

If you are not your body then what are you? If you are not your mind then what are you? Are you not that which observes both?

If you think this is unimportant then you need to bring into question what you think is important. To me, everyone is important and everyone should at least have access to this knowledge.

Your mind and your body are your 'accumulations' and unfortunately your body takes its lead from your mind. Thus if you are miserable, because of your mind, what's that doing to your body?

We all make the mistake of living in the mind instead of living in the now.

So does it really matter if your body dies? In one sense – no, because it's not what you are. But in another sense – yes, because you can only interact with this environment if you have a body of the same frequency as it.

Why would you not want to interact with this last kingdom? Rejuvenating your body is the height of your evolutionary expression.

Your mind is based in the past and it's an accumulation of all that you've entertained and judged – thus it's full of rubbish and it can only rejuvenate your body if it's cleaned out. It takes a pristine mind to ascend, which comes from taking *The Impeccable Journey*. This is a journey that takes many years. It's best you get started.

We must work at purging our minds of all limitations (throwing out all of those sandbags), because every limitation can be seen as a source of bodily decay. This is what ascension and immortality is and it's within the grasp of everyone.

There is no loss in doing this journey and if we do it, not only will we become more pleasant and more loving, we will have endeavoured to evolve ourselves and nobody can dispute that.

I hope you have enjoyed this work of mine and it has made your Spiritual journey somewhat clearer. If so, please suggest this book to your friends ~ Gary Bate

Other books by Gary Bate

We are here to know ourselves
The Question Is
Soul Completion

Links on www.whatstress.com